Leseverstehen in der Sekundarstufe II

Lesen gehört neben Schreiben und Rechnen zu den grundlegenden Kulturfertigkeiten und ist zentrale Kompetenz zur Aneignung der Welt. So ist die Lesekompetenz auch nicht nur für die Kommunikation im schulischen (und später dann im beruflichen) Leben der Schülerinnen und Schüler bedeutsam, sondern auch für deren soziale und private Interaktionen, sei es beim Lesen von Zeitungen, Zeitschriften und Büchern zum Erwerb von Faktenwissen, bei der privaten Lektüre, beim Lesen von Mails und Blogs etc. Auch wenn sich die Art des Lesens und die Lesetexte im Zeitalter des Internets verändert haben, so bleibt doch das Lesen selbst eine unverzichtbare Komponente des Kommunikationsprozesses.
Die Schulung des Leseverstehens im Englischunterricht (EU) nimmt dementsprechend eine zentrale Rolle ein. In der Sekundarstufe II sollen die Schüler und Schülerinnen aufbauend auf der Arbeit in der Sekundarstufe I selbstständig mit komplexeren, längeren und thematisch nicht mehr nur vertrauten Texten umgehen und sie als Grundlage für anspruchsvollere Fragestellungen nutzen können.
Dabei wird die Fähigkeit, einzelne Wörter und Sätze zu lesen und im Textzusammenhang zu verstehen, im Fremdsprachenunterricht systematisch und konsequent aufgebaut und geschult.
Vielen Lehrerinnen und Lehrern stellt sich daher häufig die Frage, wie dieser Forderung im Unterricht Rechnung getragen werden kann.
Das vorliegende Heft aus der Reihe *Teaching Skills* macht ein doppeltes Angebot:

- Die folgenden Einleitungsseiten geben einen praxisbezogenen Überblick über die Fertigkeit „Leseverstehen“. Neben grundsätzlichen Überlegungen zu den Zielen und den methodischen Anforderungen an die systematische Schulung der Kompetenz werden Aufgabenformate und ihre Verwendung in den Übungen erläutert.
- Die daran anschließenden Kopiervorlagen (KV) lassen sich flexibel im Unterricht einsetzen. Mit Hilfe dieser Arbeitsblätter können die Schülerinnen und Schüler Teilfertigkeiten üben und damit ihre *reading skills* insgesamt verbessern. Begleitende Kurztexte geben Hilfen und Hinweise und unterstützen so die Schülerinnen und Schüler. Die Texte orientieren sich inhaltlich an zentralen Themen der gymnasialen Oberstufe.

So strebt das Heft zweierlei an. Zum einen will es die Unterrichtenden beim oberstufengerechten Vermitteln der Kompetenz „Leseverstehen“ unterstützen und ihre *TEACHING skills* stärken. Zum anderen möchte es dazu beitragen, die sprachliche Kompetenz der Lernenden zu verbessern und damit auch deren Chance, in Prüfungssituationen zu bestehen, in denen sie diese Kompetenz beweisen sollen: *teaching SKILLS*.

Die Integration der Schulung des Leseverstehens in den Unterricht

Moderne Oberstufenlehrwerke bieten in der Regel im Rahmen ihrer thematischen Einheiten auch Materialien zum Kompetenztraining an, unter anderem zum Leseverstehen. Man kann daher davon ausgehen, dass die lesende Aufnahme von Inhalten zum Unterrichtsprogramm gehört. Allerdings tritt in der Unterrichtspraxis bei diesen lehrwerksintegrierten Materialien häufig die systematische Schulung der Leseverstehenskompetenz gegenüber der jeweils damit verbundenen inhaltlich-thematischen Auseinandersetzung mit dem Text in den Hintergrund.
Die in diesem Band angebotenen Texte und die zugehörigen KV lassen sich zentralen Themenbereichen der Oberstufenarbeit im Fach Englisch zuordnen, wobei jedoch das Hauptaugenmerk weniger auf dem jeweiligen Thema als vielmehr auf der Schulung des Leseverstehens und seiner spezifischen Anforderungen liegt

In der Sekundarstufe II gilt es, die im Laufe der Sek I eingeübten Fähigkeiten mit jeweils deutlich *methodischer* Schwerpunktsetzung auszubauen und die Verfahren, mit denen die Schülerinnen und Schüler sich beim Verstehen unterschiedlicher Textsorten selbst helfen können, zu erweitern und zu verankern.

Die KV sollen diesen Lehr- und Lernprozess in dreifacher Hinsicht unterstützen:

- beim Üben und Festigen der Fähigkeiten, Texte zu lesen und deren Inhalt, Struktur, Intention und sprachliche Gestaltung zu erkennen;
- beim Vorbereiten auf eine Überprüfung des Leseverstehens durch klassische Testformate (Multiple Choice, Multiple Matching, True/False/Citing, *gap filling* ...);
- beim Ausbau der Fähigkeit, die gelesenen Texte und die Ergebnisse des Leseprozesses als Grundlage für weitere textanalytische Verfahren (mündlich oder schriftlich) zu nutzen.

Leseverstehenskompetenz im Fremdsprachenunterricht

Leseverstehen gehört – wie das Hörverstehen – zu den rezeptiven Fertigkeiten. Trotzdem ist Lesen ein aktiver Prozess, nämlich die stumme Interaktion eines Lesers mit einem Text. Während des Lesens denkt der Leser nach über die Bedeutung einzelner Wörter, über das Gelesene insgesamt. Er setzt dabei den Text bzw. die Informationen eines Textes in Beziehung zu seinem bereits vorhandenen Wissen, entwickelt bestimmte Erwartungen an den weiteren Gang einer Geschichte, eines Textes, versucht zu antizipieren, was der Text noch zu bieten hat und entscheidet schließlich, ob er den Text interessant oder langweilig findet.
Ebenfalls grundlegend für das Textverständnis ist die Tatsache, dass jeder Text für einen bestimmten Zweck und mit Blick auf bestimmte Rezipienten geschrieben wurde, was Inhalt und Stil des Textes beeinflusst. Aber auch auf der Seite des Rezipienten (Lesers) gibt es verschiedene Absichten, z. B. das Lesen zum Vergnügen oder das schnelles Überfliegen einer Fernsehzeitung um herauszufinden, wann die Lieblingssendung wiederholt wird, oder das Lesen einer Anleitung, um ein Möbelstück zusammenzubauen, und nicht zuletzt das intensive Lesen, um Wissen zu erweitern oder um zu den Aussagen des Textes Stellung zu nehmen.
Der Aufbau von Lesekompetenz ist im schulischen Fremdsprachenlernen ein jahrelanger Prozess, den der Gemeinsame europäische Referenzrahmen (GeR) für die unterschiedlichen Stufen in einer allgemeinen Skala für das Lesen abbildet (vgl. Seite 4 oben).

Es gibt zwar unter Umständen auch für Muttersprachler durchaus einen Bedarf, die Lesefähigkeit zu verbessern, aber in Bezug auf die Leseabsicht haben wir unterschiedliche Lesestrategien internalisiert und nutzen sie zumeist unbewusst. Dagegen wird das Lesen in der Fremdsprache mit unterschiedlichen Absichten erst dann als selbstständig und mühelos empfunden, wenn wir als Leser möglichst souverän bestimmte Lesestrategien beherrschen, die uns nämlich helfen, mit dem Ziel zu lesen, das wir uns selbst gesetzt haben, z. B. Herausfiltern des Wesentlichen oder bestimmter Details.

Diese Lesestrategien lassen sich grob in zwei Arten unterteilen:

Expeditious reading – schnelles/überfliegendes Lesen

- *skimming* überfliegendes Lesen – um einen Überblick über das Wesentliche zu erhalten und/oder um zu entscheiden, ob der Text genau gelesen werde muss, um eine bestimmte Fragestellung/Aufgabe bearbeiten zu können; zeitlich begrenzt (→ KV 2)
- *scanning* suchendes , interessengeleitetes, selektives Lesen – die Suche nach bestimmten vorgegebenen oder selbst gewählten Schlüsselwörtern, Eigennamen, Jahreszahlen u.Ä.; zeitlich begrenzt (→ KV 3)

Leseverstehen allgemein	
C2	Kann praktisch alle Arten geschriebener Texte verstehen und kritisch interpretieren (einschließlich abstrakte, strukturell komplexe oder stark umgangssprachliche literarische oder nichtliterarische Texte). Kann ein breites Spektrum langer und komplexer Texte verstehen und dabei feine stilistische Unterschiede und implizite Bedeutungen erfassen.
C1	Kann lange, komplexe Texte im Detail verstehen, auch wenn diese nicht dem eigenen Spezialgebiet angehören, sofern schwierige Passagen mehrmals gelesen werden können.
B2	Kann sehr selbstständig lesen, Lesestil und -tempo verschiedenen Texten und Zwecken anpassen und geeignete Nachschlagewerke selektiv benutzen. Verfügt über einen großen Lesewortschatz, hat aber möglicherweise Schwierigkeiten mit seltener gebrauchten Wendungen.
B1	Kann unkomplizierte Sachtexte über Themen, die mit den eigenen Interessen und Fachgebieten in Zusammenhang stehen, mit befriedigendem Verständnis lesen. Kann kurze, einfache Texte zu vertrauten, konkreten Themen verstehen, in denen gängige alltags- oder berufsbezogene Sprache verwendet wird.
A2	Kann kurze, einfache Texte lesen und verstehen, die einen sehr frequenten Wortschatz und einen gewissen Anteil international bekannter Wörter enthalten.
A1	Kann sehr kurze, einfache Texte Satz für Satz lesen und verstehen, indem er/sie bekannte Namen, Wörter und einfachste Wendungen heraussucht und, wenn nötig, den Text mehrmals liest.

Gemeinsamer Europäischer Referenzrahmen, 2001, Seite 74–75

Careful reading – genaues Lesen zum Auffinden von Text- und Gliederungsstrukturen und Stilelementen, die zur Erschließung des Textes bzw. zum Entschlüsseln der Botschaften im Text relevant erscheinen (→ Überblick auf KV 1)

Folgende Operationen werden dann beim Lesen durchgeführt:

- *reading for main ideas (and supporting detail) / for overall idea* (→ KV 4)
- *recognizing text genre, discourse structure, structure of argumentative texts* (→ KV 5–10)
- *making inferences* (→ KV 11)
- *decoding (word recognition and decoding the meaning of unknown words and structures)* (→ KV 12, auch KV 9)

Das Erlernen und Üben dieser Strategien wird in der Sekundarstufe I begonnen und in der Sekundarstufe II fortgesetzt, wobei dann stärkeres Gewicht gelegt wird auf

- die Festigung und Erweiterung der Methoden im Hinblick auf die Erschließung der Textstruktur,
- die Entschlüsselung des Stils,
- das Lesen zwischen den Zeilen,
- das Füllen von Leerstellen.

Schulung des Leseverstehens im Unterricht

Auch in der Fremdsprache wird der Leseprozess vom Leser ständig (unbewusst oder bewusst) überwacht, werden Modifizierungen der Lesestrategie vorgenommen, wird das Textverständnis angepasst, je weiter man den Text liest und versteht.

Um diesen Prozess zu unterstützen, ist es sinnvoll, in drei Schritten vorzugehen:

1. **Vorbereitung auf den Leseprozess:**
   - Bewusstmachung der Intention des Lesens
   - Entscheidung für die adäquate Lesestrategie
   - Ausnutzen der Hinweise, die der Text in Form von Überschriften, Bildern, Absätzen, gestellten Aufgaben gibt (*text mapping*)
   - Aktivierung von Weltwissen
   - Aktivierung von Wissen und Kenntnissen über Satzstrukturen und Lexik
   - Ausnutzen der Hinweise und Empfehlungen in den erläuternden Boxes der KV
2. **Aktivitäten und mentale Prozesse, die den Lese- und Verstehensprozess unterstützen:**
   - gezieltes Markieren des Textes
   - Anfertigen von Notizen und Paraphrasen
   - Gliederung des Textes
   - Anwenden von Worterschließungsstrategien
   - Erkennen und Entschlüsseln impliziter Aussagen
   - Ausfüllen von Leerstellen
   - ständiges Überprüfen und Anpassen des Textverständnisses
3. **Auseinandersetzung mit Struktur, Gestaltung und Aussagen des Textes in mündlicher oder schriftlicher Form**

Einsatz der Kopiervorlagen und Arbeitsweise

Die Kopiervorlagen lassen sich in unterschiedlicher Weise im Unterricht verwenden. Sie eignen sich sowohl für die Arbeit mit der gesamten Lerngruppe als auch zur Binnendifferenzierung, d.h. für Phasen des individuellen Arbeitens und Übens.
Auf jeder KV finden sich kurze Begleittexte, in denen die Lernenden auf das jeweilige Material bzw. auf einzelne Anforderungen in den Aufgaben bezogene methodische Hinweise erhalten. Aus der Anordnung der Tipps auf den Seiten ergibt sich, wann die Schülerinnen und Schüler sie sinnvollerweise rezipieren sollten. Tipps zum jeweiligen Leseverhalten sollten unmittelbar vor dem Lesen zur Kenntnis genommen werden; andere Tipps sind aufgabenspezifisch und sollten deshalb im Zusammenhang mit der jeweils daneben stehenden Aufgabe gelesen und beherzigt werden.

Sabine Brumby-Hartogh, Heidrun Krause, Ulrike Schuh-Fricke

Essential reading methods
You don't need to read every word of a text from start to finish. There are three basic reading methods to help you work quickly and more effectively:

Skimming – quick reading to look for the gist or main points of a text, ignoring detail

Scanning – quick reading to find specific information

Careful reading – needed when you want to concentrate on precise meaning and detail
The good news is that you already possess these skills and use them every day when reading in German. Recognising when and how to use these skills with English texts will build up your ability and speed.

1 Skimming or scanning?

Discuss in class which skill you mainly use when you

a) want to know what time the football match starts (TV guide)

b) want to see if there is anything interesting on TV (TV guide)

c) want to see if a friend has replied to your email (mailbox)

d) want to find a word in the dictionary

e) want to re-read your lesson notes quickly before an exam

f) want to read an article on the internet to see if it is relevant to your current research

2 Skimming

Skim the titles and descriptions of the following books to find out what they are about, underlining or highlighting words that give you the information (cf. the example given in A).

A ***Wild Swim***
by Kate Rew & Dominick Tyler
An inspiring guide with photos so stunning you'll be itching to dig out your swimming costume. This tour of Britain presents 300 swimming locations, from waterfalls to Jacuzzis, caves to rivers; there's something for everyone, whether you're a child wanting a paddle or a seasoned cold-water swimmer.
RRP [regular retail price] *£14.99*
Our Price £9.99 **Save £5**

B ***Eyewitness Decade***
by Roger Tooth
This beautiful book tells the story of the first ten years of the noughties through more than 100 awe-inspiring photographs. All the major events are captured, from the installation of the London Eye in 2000 right through to Obama's inauguration in 2009, along with amazing, funny and moving images portraying human ingenuity and the quirkier side of life.
RRP £25 Our Price £17.50 **Save £7.50**

C ***Chicken Coops for the Soul & The Allotment Keeper's Handbook***
by Julia Hollander & Jane Perrone
For happy hens and glorious veg, look no further than these two great guides to self-sufficiency. Follow Julia Hollander through the trials and tribulations of keeping chickens in a small urban garden and allow Jane Perrone to guide you with the best tips for allotment management to ensure a bountiful harvest.
RRP £27.98 Our Price £16
Save £11.98

D

Dadcando
by Chris Barnardo
Brimful of magical and creative ideas to try at home, from building a spaceship to kitchen-sink science experiments, *Dadcando* is the ideal gift for any father keen to spend quality time with his kids. It also includes bags of support and advice for any father who finds himself going it alone.
RRP £14.99 Our Price £10
Save £4.99

E

Women of the Revolution
by Kira Cochrane
When hundreds gathered in 1970 for the UK's first women's liberation conference, it set in motion a frenzy of activity that transformed the way we think, act and live. This collection of articles charts the progress of feminism, and asks two fundamental questions: Who are we? Who should we be?
RRP £18.99 Our Price £14.99
Save £4

F

True North
by Martin Wainwright
Bleak landscape, abysmal weather, funny accents ... are these preconceptions of 'the north' true, or are they clichés indulged in by soft southerners? Intrepid northerner Wainwright searches through the historical record to find where they first arose, and paints a picture of what 'the north' is really like.
RRP £8.99 Our Price £6.99
Save £2

G

The Bedside Guardian 2010
by Chris Elliott
All the very best reporting from the *Guardian* providing eyewitness reports and perceptive commentary on the year, both at home and abroad. Covering politics, the environment, natural disasters, sport and entertainment, this is a fascinating read for anyone interested in current affairs.
RRP £14.99 Our Price £10
Save £4.99

H

Unknown Bown & Exposures
by Jane Bown
These two gorgeous books showcase the much-loved Jane Bown's photographs of the last sixty years, from the iconic portraits of *Exposures*, presented uncropped and in their full glory, to the non-portraiture work featured in *Unknown Bown*, which reveals a new dimension to her extraordinary talents. Together they provide a fascinating insight into the artistic development of a twentieth-century legend.
RRP £50 Our Price £30 **Save £20**

I

My Family and Other Disasters
by Lucy Mangan
One of the *Guardian*'s most popular columnists shares her unique view on life, death and everything in between in this collection of her columns. From the credit crunch to family relations, Mangan offers a wry, humorous take on modern life that will have you shaking your head in wonder and agreement.
RRP £7.99 Our Price £5.99
Save £2

3 Scanning and careful reading

Decide whether there are any books in the list above (**2**) that are suitable for someone interested in the subjects given in the left column below. To do so, first scan the words you have highlighted or underlined and then carefully read the surrounding text to check that you are making the right choice. Then, write down the book recommendation in the middle column and say why. If you do not have a recommendation, just put '—'.

Subject	**Book recommendation?**	**Why?**
family watersports	A	300 swimming locations, a child wanting a paddle
global warming		
countryside animal farming		
fatherhood and divorce		
photo journalism		
women's history		
North Pole exploration		

Skimming
Don't feel overwhelmed by the size of a text. You can start breaking down its outline structure quite quickly to give you lots of clues about its content, as well as a feeling of 'control' over it.

Skimming the outline of the text includes:
- any titles and visuals,
- the first and last paragraphs,
- the first sentences of all the other paragraphs.

This gives you immediate insight into
- the type of text,
- the tone of voice,
- how the text unfolds,
- where to scan for specific information later,
- the writer's message.

1 Look at this heading of a newspaper article and answer the questions:

> The new India
> **How did India do it?**
> The rise of a new global force

What seems to be the subject of the text? ______________________

What does the reader learn about the subject of the text?

____

What text type could this be? (Several answers are possible.)

☐ a) expository text
☐ b) descriptive text
☐ c) argumentative text
☐ d) persuasive text
☐ e) instructive text

What do you think the main focus of the text is going to be?

☐ a) economy
☐ b) war
☐ c) politics
☐ d) sport
☐ e) fashion

2 Now look at the text below. Skim the whole of the first and last paragraphs, then skim the first sentences of all the other paragraphs and highlight them with a coloured marker.

Highlighting and marking
Using a highlighter to mark the first sentences of paragraphs turns the text into a 'list' of topics and is a helpful reminder later when you start scanning for specific information.
Some highlighted sentences will show you that you might need to check the previous paragraph for the information you want.
If a paragraph is very long, it's a good idea to also skim the last sentence. If you want to mark something there as well, circle or underline it.

The new India

How did India do it?

The rise of a new global force

By Aditya Chakrabortty

Outsiders see India as a new power on the rise; Indians, on the other hand, talk about a revival, a restoration of fortunes. They point out that in the 18th century, India had the biggest economy in the world, larger than all of western Europe and the Americas put together. Even after independent India came to be stereotyped as a land of urban slums and rural poverty, there was a feeling that inside this poor country, there was a rich one struggling to get out.

In the past two decades, it has finally emerged, thanks to growing industries (most notably IT) and government policies to cut regulation. Much of this success can be traced back to Jawaharlal Nehru. As prime minister of India from its birth in 1947 until his death in 1964, he wanted it to be not only free of foreign rule, but self-sufficient economically. His answer? Heavy industry, state-directed investment, and five-year economic plans.

Historians have not been kind to Nehru. He cuts an unfashionable figure with quaint enthusiasms (Steel smelting! Hydro-electric dams!). Yet the inconvenient truth for today's free-market-loving India is that the foundations for its success were laid by Nehru's socialist economics.

Those booming subcontinental IT firms, and even the US's Silicon Valley (which recruits so many of the subcontinent's software engineers), prosper thanks to Nehru's creation of elite technological and business schools. Neither Pakistan nor Bangladesh made such far-sighted investment and that, along with political instability, largely accounts for their failure to take off.

All this state intervention had a downside: red tape that grew like bindweed. A carmaker wanting to make more vehicles in its own factory needed permission from a bureaucrat, which meant forms, permits and pleading. The Licence Raj, as it was known, nearly stifled the life out of India's private sector.

But in 1991 a cash-strapped Indian government was forced to ask other countries for a loan. Donors insisted that it open up its economy – both to its own private sector and to foreign competition. The Licence Raj was out: from now on the government would intervene less, regulate less – generally do less.

And India started to change. Take that staple of commercial life: the phone call. 'In the old days,' says Deepak Lalwani, an Indian-born stockbroker now based in London, 'if a Bombay businessman wanted to phone Delhi he had to book a line and wait a few hours.' The call would then be upgraded to urgent. A couple more hours would pass. Then, says Lalwani, 'The booking would at last be given "lightning" status.' Another hour and at last the conversation could begin, having by now accrued all the ceremony of a state summit. Today, an exec making a call would not only not need to book; he or she would probably use a mobile instead. In 2000, Indians bought 3m mobiles; this June [2007] alone they bought 7.3m. That does still leave almost 80% of Indians with no phone at all, however. In villages, where the vast majority of the population lives, there are barely any cellular networks.

This sums up what is right and wrong with India's embrace of freer markets. It has been a boon for the educated, middle class, largely city-dwelling minority able to take advantage of it – and of little help to anyone else. The economy is growing at nearly double its historic rate, but this has been a jobless boom, creating better jobs, but not new jobs, and concentrated in services (all those software firms, back offices and call centres).

By contrast, China, often put in the same bracket, has focused on employment-creating manufacturing and developing infrastructure. And while Delhi politicians see their job as merely getting out of the private sector's way, Beijing remains heavily involved in economic decisions. How big is the boom in India's economy? About as big as the US. That's the size of India's new middle class, the main beneficiaries of the new regime. By 2010, there will be 300m of them: equal to the US in population size – and perhaps in taste. If you want evidence, drive an hour out of Delhi to Gurgaon, a town sometimes called the centre of the new India. The main drag is called Mall Road. A bit further along is a housing estate called Malibu Town. It has its own security guards, a golf club and roads with names such as Pine Drive. It is pleasant enough, but it bears little resemblance to the rest of the country. How to narrow that difference is India's new problem.

3 Using the information you have skimmed and highlighted or otherwise marked, answer the following questions. Skim the text once more if necessary.

a) What tone of voice does the writer use when describing India?

unbiased and factual ☐

admiring and persuasive ☐

amused and sarcastic ☐

b) What text type is it? Was your assumption based on the heading (cf. **1**) correct?

c) The text seems to split into two sections. What are they? Gie the line numbers.

First section: ll. 0–__________, second section: ll. __________–52.

d) Give the two sections simple titles.

First section: ______________________________

Second section: ______________________________

e) Say which parts of the text you would study more closely to find more information about

- India's old problematic bureaucracy
- India's new problems
- How India received outside help
- The size of India's new economy
- Nehru's politics

f) What does the writer seem to think is a problem in the new India?

differences in class ☐

differences in housing standards ☐

differences in living standards ☐

4 Looking again at your highlighted sentences and at your answers to **3**, find the following ideas and say in which order they appear in the text.

- [ ] a) Capitalist prosperity has grown from socialist beginnings.
- [ ] b) Foreign financial intervention forced important changes on the Indian economy.
- [ ] c) The new economy has not created more employment.
- [1] d) Indians feel that history has repeated itself.
- [ ] e) Education was the basis for success in the computer industry.
- [ ] f) The increase in wealth has only improved life for one class of Indians.

Looking for specific information
Once you have *skimmed* a text and have an idea what the text is about and where to find certain kinds of information, you are ready to *scan* for specific information that you may need for answering particular questions.
Quickly run your eyes over the text to look for names, dates, keywords or for synonyms connected to the idea in the question.
Scan the whole text. You may find a lot of relevant information in one area but that doesn't mean there isn't more somewhere else.
Keep checking back to the exact wording of the question to ensure you are not tricked into including related but incorrect answers.
Paraphrase your answer if necessary. If you are asked for an explanation, you may need to change the order or form of the words you find – but be careful not to change the meaning.
Do not give the same information twice in your answer just because the idea is expressed in two different ways in the text.

1 a) Skim the following text.

Most places develop tourism because of its economic potential: it creates jobs; brings in new money; is relatively clean; and has minimal start-up costs. In addition to these monetary benefits, it can also help conserve national heritage, protect the environment and contribute to an improvement in the quality of life and well-being of local communities.
However, tourism has a down-side, and like any other socio-economic activity, it carries with it costs as well as benefits. Tourism is seasonal by nature, and thus so are many of the jobs. It can lead to local inflation and profits can 'leak' away to external suppliers and proprietors. It can also put a strain on local infrastructure and services, enhance social problems, increase pollution and lead to overcrowding and traffic congestion in different environments.
Thus, like any other industry, the development of tourism requires a sound knowledge of both the opportunities and constraints it represents to a destination. If planners and managers are to develop and maintain a sustainable and successful tourism industry, they will need to be more aware of, and understand tourism's impacts. In doing so they should be in a better position to consider the trade-offs necessary to achieve this goal.

12 *enhance sth.* intensify sth., increase sth.
20 *trade-off (infml)* concession, compromise

Conciseness and accuracy
When filling in a table you will often need to categorise information. Study the categories carefully to make sure you know exactly what type of information you are looking for.
Be concise as well as accurate in your answers – don't use too many or too few words.
Make sure you follow a writer's opinion or explanation to its conclusion before using any information, otherwise your answer could be incomplete.

b) Complete the following table with information from the text in **1** a). Your entries should be in note form, not necessarily whole sentences.

	Possible benefits of tourism	**Possible disadvantages of tourism**
Natural surroundings		
Employment		
Money		
Living conditions		

c) Check with a partner. If there are any small differences in what you have written, discuss which answer most accurately represents the information given in the text.

d) Which term (consisting of two words) sums up what, according to the text, needs to be considered in order to create successful tourism in an area?

2 a) Skim the following text.

Assaulted in broad daylight

We see on average 3,500 brand images a day, fleetingly or full on, from TVs, magazines, newspapers and, increasingly, on our computers, tablets and smartphones. But we see them, too, on billboards and buses, in taxis, on the tube, on trains and in stations, and even in hospitals and schools. Is there a difference and should we do anything about it? The difference is choice. We can decide what stations to watch, websites to look at or magazines to buy. But we can't choose not to be in public spaces, to walk down streets, get on buses or the tube or reasonably expect our children not to do the same. So where is the harm in outdoor advertising and should we be allowed to choose?

The harm is the same as for other advertising. Images of perfect bodies, flash new cars or cheap fast food are researched, tested, designed and plastered everywhere to make you feel anxious, insecure or become obese. Adverts are not there to inform but to sell one thing: un-happiness. They work because they make us dissatisfied with what we've got or what we look like. They make us want the next new thing, until of course the next new thing comes along. They help sow the seeds of insecurity, humiliation, debt, brand bullying at school and, through the remorseless use of resources they inspire, they threaten the planet.

To those who say 'just say no' I would suggest they look at themselves and their wardrobe and the infinite choices they make to belong to one particular tribe and then look around them at the way in which everyone else is doing the same. The advertising industry exists to ensure it becomes culturally and emotionally impossible to refuse.

And the thing about outdoor advertising is that you can't not look and you can't escape. Surely we should be able to say enough is enough. The freedom from unwanted and damaging advertising should trump the freedom to sell. If outdoor adverts were banned, our towns and cities would be transformed. We would see more of the sky and our urban landscape. And our minds would have that bit more space for ideas, plans, love or just to daydream. Some sites could be used for great public art, information and inspiring poems and quotes. Not just another airbrushed perfect body meant to make us feel inadequate.

[1] *fleetingly* very quickly
[22] *trump sth. (v)* triumph over sth., win against sth.

b) Read the following questions, then scan the text to find the answers. Check your answers in class.

Advertising has harmful effects. Which four adjectives from the text describe how advertising can make people feel?

________________ ________________

________________ ________________

According to the text, what is the main difference between outdoor advertising and other forms of advertising?

____

____

To fully understand an argumentative text and be able to answer questions on it, you need to clearly recognize three elements:

- The **topic**, i.e. the subject of the text;
- the **main idea**, i.e. the strongest idea expressed about the topic. Generally, writers mention several ideas about their topic, so be careful. You have to decide which idea is the strongest or which one covers all the others;
- the **message**, i.e. what the writer wants to point out to the reader and the reason he or she wrote the text. The message may either be clearly stated or only implied. Parts of the message can be 'buried' in other areas of the text, so you may need to re-skim in order to make sure that you have identified the whole message.

1 Study the sentences below and complete the explanations.

a) Tom likes eating ice-cream, biscuits, cream cakes and chocolate.

Topic: *Things Tom likes eating*

Main idea: *He likes chocolate flavours.* No, because ______________________

____

____

He doesn't like salty food. No, because ______________________

____

____

____

He likes sweet food. Yes, because this covers all the information.

b) He likes eating sweet food, but he is often at the dentist and has put on so much weight that he can't even run for the bus now.

Message: *He likes eating sweet food, but it is damaging his health.*

Implied message: He ______________________

____

______________________ because it is damaging his health.

2 a) Read the following beginning of an article. Highlight the topic, the main idea and the message with coloured markers and label them in the margin.

'Many big ideas have struggled over the centuries to dominate the planet,' begins the argument by Jonathon Porritt, government adviser and all-round environmental guru. 'Fascism. Communism. Democracy. Religion. But only one has achieved total supremacy. Its compulsive attractions rob its followers of reason and good sense. It has created unsustainable inequalities and threatened to tear apart the very fabric of our society. More powerful than any cause or even religion, it has reached into every corner of the globe. It is consumerism.'	

According to Porritt, the most senior adviser to the government on sustainability, we have become a generation of shopaholics. We are bombarded by advertising from every medium which persuades us that the more we consume, the better our lives will be. Shopping is equated with fun, fulfilment and self-identity. It is also, Porritt warns, killing the planet. He argues, in an interview with the *Observer*, that merely switching to 'ethical' shopping is not enough. We must shop less.	

b) Put the topic, the main idea and the message together in a sentence to identify the opinion that you think will be expressed in more detail in the rest of the article. Compare your answers in class.

____

____

____

3 Now skim the rest of the article. Highlight those passages that expand on either the topic, the main idea or the message, labelling in the margin what each one is.

Porritt, chairman of the government's Sustainable Development Commission, has concluded that consumerism is central to the threat facing the planet, cannibalising its natural resources and producing the carbon dioxide emissions which result in climate change. In a film for Channel Five, he points out that Britons throw away their own body weight in rubbish every seven weeks, with 100 million tonnes of waste pouring into the country's 12,000 landfill sites every year. If all six billion people in the world were to consume at the same level, we would need two new Earths to supply all the energy, soil, water and raw materials required. 'I think capitalism is patently unable to go on growing the size of the consumer economy for any more people in the world today because levels of consumption are already undermining life support systems on which we depend – so if we do it for any more people, the planet will go pop,' Porritt told the *Observer*. 'So in a way we don't have a choice about this: we've got to rethink the basic premise behind capitalism to make it deliver the goods. In the long run, when you really look at what happens on a planet with nine billion people and really serious constraints on the amount of carbon dioxide and other greenhouse gases that we can emit, it's almost inevitable we will learn to have more elegant, satisfying lives, consuming less. I can't see any way out of that in the long run.' Porritt, co-founder of Forum For The Future, Britain's leading sustainable development charity, believes that consumerism has taken over our lives almost unnoticed. 'Shopping has become a recreational activity,' he continued. 'There's a lot of evidence that people really do see shopping now as an amenity pastime. We're well beyond the time where shopping was just a way of	

transacting what you needed in life. It's now all about identity and status and recreation and companionship, even about meaning in people's lives. There's always been a "keeping up with the Joneses" type thing, but it's now almost universalised and there is a sense of buying to be more like something or to get the image of somebody, particularly with clothes or branded goods, where there's very much that sense of, "If I buy something with this name on it, maybe a little bit of the magic of that name will rub off on me and I'll be a better person", whereas we all know you're exactly the same person just waiting to go out and make your next branded purchase.' […] He denies that he is advocating a return to the austerity and rationing last seen during and just after the Second World War, although he describes low air fares as 'ludicrous' and warns a sacrifice will have to be made to reduce carbon emissions. 'I know for sure that if we ever had a golden age, as far as most people are concerned, it's been over the last 50 years. That's the period of the greatest prosperity for the greatest number of people, so I don't have any nostalgia for past eras where life was simpler but more primitive. I don't talk about going back to anything, I talk about using technology a great deal more intelligently and efficiently to continue to give us a very high quality of life with a fraction of the environmental cost. 'We need "sustainability literacy", enabling people to see what the costs of living in a certain way really look like. We're blind to a lot of that. When people take holidays in far-flung places they very rarely think about the impact of hundreds of thousands of tourists descending on some destination somewhere in the world. We've just got to get wiser to what happens when we enjoy the perks of this life.'	

[31] *undermine sth.* weaken sth.
[37] *constraint on sth.* limit of sth.
[50] *keep up with the Joneses (infml)* copy one's friends' and neighbours' lifestyles
[59] *advocate sth.* argue for sth., recommend sth.
[61] *ludicrous* ridiculous

4 Skim ll. 18–77 of the article to complete the following list of things the writer says we need to do in the future to protect the environment.

- Rethink the basic premise behind capitalism
- ______________________________
- ______________________________
- ______________________________
- ______________________________
- ______________________________

5 Discuss in class whether the message the writer has given by the end of the article is different from the one he presented at the beginning (cf. **2**).

1 Read the text below and decide where to put the following terms in the margin:

- background / setting the scene
- cause of problem
- problem
- details of problem
- opposite viewpoint
- results / implications

The terms may refer to a single line, to a few lines or to a whole paragraph.

> **The structure of argumentative texts**
> Argumentative texts often deal with a particular problem, and they contain characteristic elements: the writer describes the problem in some detail, looks at the causes and effects, discusses people's views of the problem, etc. Being familiar with these elements and identifying them quickly helps you to understand what the text is about and how it is structured.

Before my mum got pregnant, we got on really well. She was always good company and helped me with lots of things. But then the baby arrived about three months ago. And mum doesn't seem to notice my existence any more! She is always busy and when the baby finally falls asleep, she disappears for a rest too. I can understand that she is tired. And I know the baby is helpless and relies on her for everything, so she doesn't really have a choice. But if things don't change soon, I think I'll be glad to get out! My home life just isn't the same anymore.	

2 Compare in class how you annotated the text. Then answer the following questions:

a) Does the writer suggest or hint at a solution to the problem he or she describes?

b) Does he or she give a warning if a solution is not found?

3 Read the following headline and sub-heading of a newspaper article and answer the questions.

> **The erosion by stealth and wealth of *Shakespeare in the Park*'s great ideal**
> This amazing, 50-year tradition of performing Shakespeare free for New Yorkers risks becoming mere corporate entertainment

a) What is *Shakespeare in the Park* and what is its 'great ideal'?

b) How can you tell from the headline and sub-heading that the following text is going to deal with a problem?

4 Now read the article and put the terms that you used before (cf. **1**) in the appropriate places in the margin. You may have to use a term more than once.

Oppressive, overcrowded New York is not much fun in the summer, but among theater-goers one institution makes the sweltering months worth waiting for. Shakespeare in the Park begins its 50th season this week, and in the past half-century the festival, managed by the Public Theater, has matured from an improbable experiment into a city birthright. Audiences are still filling the Delacorte Theater in Central Park, sited perfectly amid the trees and the water. And amazingly, the tickets are still free – though you may have to get in line at daybreak, or even earlier. […] But in this anniversary season, there is already something to worry about. More and more, Shakespeare in the Park is tending away from the bedrock principle on which it was founded: that all tickets should be free. Joe Papp, the secular saint who fought for years to build a theater in Central Park, was able to rely mostly on the city government and a collection of munificent New Yorkers to fund his new theater. These days, however, Shakespeare in the Park receives its primary support from large corporations such as Bank of America and Bloomberg – and they want to be thanked. Although the Public is cagey about just how many tickets go to corporate sponsors, its former executive director said that, on an individual night, the percentage of seats allocated to donors can hit 30%. On its website, the Public is not shy about the exchange rate between donations and tickets. 'Entertain clients or employees this summer in Central Park!' it cheerfully proposes, and the more you give, the more seats the ushers will rope off for you. Not only that, the house will provide a convenient 'VIP entrance' for you and your colleagues, in case you were worried you might have to mix with the lowly bardolators who camped out all night. And naturally, you should feel free to take the gift off your taxes – since this isn't a purchase, this is charity. […] It's easy to call this a necessary evil. A theater where 70% of tickets are free – and Joe Papp would surely agree here – is better than one where 100% are not. And I certainly don't begrudge the Public the money. Unlike Europe's leading houses, like the National Theatre in London or the Royal Dramatic Theater in Stockholm, the Public has to do all the work of a national producer with none of the government funding. But the establishment of a market for tickets – this much 'charity' for this many seats – does more than just let a few well-off people pay with money instead of time. It's much more harmful than that. It cheapens the entire institution, and it erodes the thing that makes it uniquely valuable: its openness. When Papp began his push for a permanent home	

for what was then called the New York Shakespeare Festival, he had to fight for years with city authorities, which insisted he charge admission. But for him, even a quarter was too much. […] Would Shakespeare in the Park have survived for 50 years had tickets cost $5 or $10 in 1962? I suspect not, though I can't be certain. But what is unquestionable is that the institution would never have achieved its position as a uniquely civic theater, one where plays 400 years old can speak directly to American society. Papp made a commitment to a Shakespeare in American English when most other theaters were either avoiding his work entirely or doing it in a sub-Olivier jaw. He pioneered color-blind casting decades before it was commonplace: James Earl Jones played Othello here, but he also played King Lear. But what made all that matter was the audience he assembled: younger, less experienced, and from across the city and the nation. At the Delacorte, Shakespeare not only spoke to America but looked like it. The individuals who buy their way in are missing that civic component of Shakespeare in the Park. For them, a play outside is just another summer trifle. But the corporations whose logos adorn the programs and the posters are doing something more destructive. They are using the egalitarian values of Shakespeare in the Park to legitimate their own perpetuation of inequality, and in the process are destroying the very egalitarianism they came to feed upon. A democratic institution is not supposed to have a VIP entrance. Shakespeare in the Park still has a relevance that few other arts institutions enjoy. But if Bank of America and their confreres have their way with it, it may recede from our central stage to just a bunch of poor players signifying nothing. I have great admiration for Oskar Eustis, whose heart is unquestionably in the right place. But if we want to guarantee another 50 years for Shakespeare in the Park, perhaps this is the summer to occupy Arden.	

[22] *cagey* secretive, not wanting to give sb. information
[32] *bardolator* (here) strong admirer of Shakespeare (often called 'the bard' = 'Barde')
[56] *civic* of or belonging to a city
[80] *Oskar Eustis* artistic director of the Public Theater
[83] *occupy Arden* (here) protest against the selling of tickets for Shakespeare in the Park

5 Compare your results in class and answer the following questions:

a) In the writer's opinion, what is the problem and what causes it?

b) According to the writer, what are the results and implications of the problem?

1 Read the following excerpt from a *Guardian* article, ignoring the numbered deletions. Then do the task below.

> **Isolating the argument**
> Writers often use examples to support and illustrate the points they make in an argument. These examples can help you, but they can also distract you in the beginning when you are trying to follow the writer's argument. Therefore, if you recognise examples – lists, anecdotes, stories and descriptions – when initially skimming a text, try ignoring them in order to isolate and understand the bare argument. You can always refer back to them later.

Do we in Britain suffer from theatrical xenophobia? I used to think so. As a young critic, I was appalled by how little we saw outside the familiar Anglo-American rep, and our snooty attitude to visiting companies. Now in 2012, as we relish the delights of the Cultural Olympiad and London's World Stages season – to mention only the most high-profile projects – I sometimes wonder if the pendulum hasn't swung rather far in the opposite direction. Do we now have an uncritical acceptance of anything foreign?
That certainly wasn't true when I set out. [...] ①
I exaggerate only slightly: British theatre was marked by its cosy insularity and its fog-isolates-Europe attitude towards the continental mainland. As for Asia and Africa, they barely registered on the radar. All that changed because of the emergence of a whole new generation of writers and directors, both well-travelled and culturally omnivorous. [...] ② We have shed our xenophobia and our theatre is all the richer for it. But I suspect we now operate a double-standard, especially when it comes to the wilder excesses of directors' theatre: OK if it's foreign, to be rubbished if it's British. [...] ③ In short, I think we need to be as critically discriminating about visiting theatre as we are about our own and avoid falling into the trap of assuming that anything from abroad possesses some magic elixir denied to our own prosaic playwright-led process. I'm happy as Larry that we have banished our cultural xenophobia. I'm just anxious we don't replace it with a naïve acceptance of anything exotically foreign.

[2] *snooty (infml)* arrogant
[8] *insularity* disconnectedness
[11] *omnivorous* [ɒmˈnɪvərəs] (here) greedy

The article aims to

☐ a) highlight xenophobia in British theatre.
☐ b) warn of a new danger facing British theatre.
☐ c) chart the recent history of British theatre.

Check your answer in class and be ready to explain your choice.

2 In the text above, the examples have been left out in order to isolate the writer's bare argument. Match the following three passages of examples to gaps 1, 2 and 3 in the text.

a) The poet and playwright Tony Harrison deserves an immense amount of credit for his pioneering versions of *The Misanthrope* and *Phaedra Britannica*. Declan Donnellan and Nick Ormerod at the touring company Cheek by Jowl opened a window on the world with their productions of plays by Racine, Corneille, Calderon and Ostrovsky. Stephen Daldry and Laurence Boswell at west London's Gate theatre, Jonathan Kent and Ian McDiarmid at the Almeida and Michael Grandage in his seasons at the Sheffield Crucible and the Donmar were also instrumental in expanding the rep. I remember Grandage saying that he hoped other work at the Crucible would pay for his risky 2004 revival of *Don Carlos*: instead it turned out to be the Schiller that audiences adored, and which the next year turned into a West End and Broadway hit.

b) The French classics, especially Racine and Corneille, were regarded as untranslatable, unplayable and theatrically arid. As for the Germans, no one bothered much with dry-as-dust Schiller, while Goethe's *Faust* was fit only for the study. We loved Chekhov, largely because we turned his plays into celebrations of the twilit pathos of the English country gentry: we studiously ignored, however, the rest of the Russian heritage and glibly assumed all modern Soviet plays were about tractors. And, while we revived the naturalistic plays of Ibsen and Strindberg, we turned a blind eye to their epic or expressionist works.

2 *arid* dry, barren
5 *glibly* (here) without thinking

c) I was thinking of two recent productions of *Macbeth* and *King John*. The former came from Poland and was seen briefly at Shakespeare's Globe as part of the World Shakespeare festival; the latter is in the RSC's current season at Stratford's Swan. Both productions made extensive use of pop culture. Both were cynical about power. Both were sexually explicit: a transvestite whore went down on Macbeth at the Globe, while Pippa Nixon's female Bastard and Alex Waldman's King John get it together at Stratford. Yet while the Polish Macbeth was greeted with whoops and cheers, Maria Aberg's King John has had a decidedly mixed reception and was dismissed as 'stupefyingly dire' in the *Independent*. Personally, I couldn't see all that much difference between the productions – both, I thought, mixed the innovative and the idiotic. I was just struck by the way a Polish director could get away with things for which a British-based one was gratuitously crucified.

8 *dire* dreadful

3 The following is an excerpt from Aravind Adiga's novel *The White Tiger* (2008). In the novel, the Indian speaker writes a series of letters to the premier of China, Wen Jiabao.

Skim the text and highlight the descriptive examples it contains. Then read each example, as well as the sentences before and after it, and underline the point the writer is making.

> **Descriptive example in novels**
> In argumentative texts, writers usually make their point clearly before or after the example. However, in novel extracts, it can be more confusing. You may *also* need to search the beginning or end of the descriptive example itself to decide what point the writer is making.

Mr Jiabao.

Sir.
When you get here, you'll be told we Indians invented everything from the Internet to hard-boiled eggs to space-ships before the British stole it all from us.
Nonsense. The greatest thing to come out of this country in the ten thousand years of its history is the Rooster Coop.
Go to Old Delhi, behind the Jama Masjid, and look at the way they keep chickens there in the market. Hundreds of pale hens and brightly coloured roosters, stuffed tightly into wire-mesh cages, packed as tightly as worms in a belly, pecking each other and shitting on each other, jostling for breathing space; the whole cage giving off a horrible stench – the stench of terrified, feathered flesh. On the wooden desk above this coop sits a grinning young butcher, showing off the flesh and organs of recently chopped-up chicken, still oleaginous with a coating of dark blood. The roosters in the coop smell the blood from above. They see the organs of their brothers lying around them. They know they're next. Yet they do not rebel. They do not try to get out of the coop.
The very same thing is done with human beings in this country. […]

Every day, on the roads of Delhi, some chauffeur is driving an empty car with a black suitcase sitting on the backseat. Inside that suitcase is a million, two million rupees; more money than that chauffeur will see in his lifetime. If he took the money he could go to America, Australia, anywhere, and start a new life. He could go inside the five-star hotels he has dreamed about all his life and only seen from the outside. He could take his family to Goa, to England. Yet he takes that black suitcase where his master wants. He puts it down where he is meant to, and never touches a rupee. Why?

Because Indians are the world's most honest people, like the prime minister's booklet will inform you?

No. It's because 99.9 per cent of us are caught in the Rooster Coop just like those poor guys in the poultry market.

The Rooster Coop doesn't always work with minuscule sums of money. Don't test your chauffeur with a rupee coin or two – he may well steal that much. But leave a million dollars in front of a servant and he won't touch a penny. [...] It's true. Every evening on the train out of Surat, where they run the world's biggest diamond-cutting and polishing business, the servants of diamond merchants are carrying suitcases full of cut diamonds that they have to give to someone in Mumbai. Why doesn't that servant take the suitcase full of diamonds? He's no Gandhi, he's human, he's you and me. But he's in the Rooster Coop. The trustworthiness of servants is the basis of the entire Indian economy.

The Great Indian Rooster Coop. Do you have something like it in China too? I doubt it, Mr Jiabao. Or you wouldn't need the Communist Party to shoot people and secret police to raid their houses at night and put them in jail like I've heard you have over there. Here in India we have no dictatorship. No secret police.

That's because we have the coop.

Never before in human history have so few owed so much to so many, Mr Jiabao. A handful of men in this country have trained the remaining 99.9 per cent – as strong, as talented, as intelligent in every way – to exist in perpetual servitude; a servitude so strong that you can put the key of his emancipation in a man's hands and he will throw it back at you with a curse. [...]

Why does the Rooster Coop work? How does it trap so many millions of men and women so effectively?

Secondly, can a man break out of the coop? What if one day, for instance, a driver took his employer's money and ran? What would his life be like?

I will answer both for you, sir.

The answer to the first question is that the pride and glory of our nation, the repository of all our love and sacrifice, the subject of no doubt considerable space in the pamphlet that the prime minister will hand over to you, the Indian family, is the reason we are trapped and tied to the coop.

The answer to the second question is that only a man who is prepared to see his family destroyed – hunted, beaten, and burned alive by the masters – can break out of the coop. That would take no normal human being, but a freak, a pervert of nature.

4 Tick the correct box. Check your answers in class.

The speaker describes a typical Indian street market to illustrate

☐ a) the horror of street life in Delhi.
☐ b) how animals are treated in India.
☐ c) how the animals accept their fate.

The speaker describes the chauffeur's journey as an example of how employees

☐ a) dream of another life.
☐ b) are trapped in a system.
☐ c) are trustworthy at work.

The speaker describes the men on the train to point out how such employees

☐ a) empower the country's financial system.
☐ b) do important jobs.
☐ c) are the same as everybody else.

The employees do not try to steal from their master because they

☐ a) are proud of their family.
☐ b) are afraid of their family.
☐ c) want to protect their family.

7 KV Breaking down paragraphs

Analysing paragraphs

If you find an argumentative text difficult to follow after skimming it, study each problematic paragraph separately and break it down into smaller sections.

- First, read the paragraph carefully and separate each point the writer makes with a text marking. Underline any words you think are important.
- Then, make sure you understand any words or phrases used to link the points and mark them.

By studying each point separately and understanding how one point is connected to the next, you will be better able to follow the line or 'shape' of the argument

When you have identified the topic and the main idea of the paragraph, you can note them in the margin to refer to later.

1 Skim the following excerpt from Nelson Mandela's autobiography *Long Walk to Freedom* (1995). Ignore, for the time being, the paragraph numbers and any underlining.

① Walter's house in Orlando was a mecca for activists and ANC members. It was a warm, welcoming place and I was often there to sample either a political discussion or Ma Sisulu's cooking. One night in 1943 I met Anton Lembede, who held Master of Arts and Bachelor of Law degrees, and A.P. Mda. From the moment I heard Lembede speak, I knew I was seeing a magnetic personality who thought in original and often startling ways. He was then one of a handful of African lawyers in the whole of South Africa and was the legal partner of the venerable Dr Pixley ka Seme, one of the founders of the ANC.

② Lembede said that Africa was a black man's continent, and it was up to Africans to reassert themselves and reclaim what was rightfully theirs. He hated the idea of the black inferiority complex and castigated what he called the worship and idolization of the West and its ideas. The inferiority complex, he affirmed, was the greatest barrier to liberation. He noted that wherever the African had been given the opportunity, he was capable of developing to the same extent as the white man, citing such African heroes as Marcus Garvey, W.E.B. Du Bois and Haile Selassie. 'The colour of my skin is beautiful,' he said, 'like the black soil of Mother Africa.' He believed blacks had to improve their own self-image before they could initiate successful mass action. He preached self-reliance and self-determination, and called his philosophy Africanism. We took it for granted that one day he would lead the ANC.

③ Lembede declared that a new spirit was stirring among the people, that ethnic differences were melting away, that young men and women thought of themselves as Africans first and foremost, not as Xhosas or Ndebeles or Tswanas. Lembede, whose father was an illiterate Zulu peasant from Natal, had trained as a teacher at Adam's College, an American Board of Missions institution. He had taught for years in the Orange Free State, learned Afrikaans, and had come to see Afrikaner nationalism as a prototype of African nationalism.

④ As Lembede later wrote in the newspaper *Inkundla ya Bantu,* an African newspaper in Natal:

> The history of modern times is the history of nationalism. Nationalism has been tested in the people's struggles and the fires of battle and found to be the only antidote against foreign rule and modern imperialism. It is for that reason that the great imperialistic powers feverishly endeavour with all their might to discourage and eradicate all nationalistic tendencies among their alien subjects; for that purpose huge and enormous sums of money are lavishly expended on propaganda against nationalism which is dismissed as 'narrow', 'barbarous', 'uncultured', 'devilish', etc. Some alien subjects become dupes of this sinister propaganda and consequently become tools or instruments of imperialism, for which great service they are highly praised by the imperialistic power and showered with such epithets as 'culture', 'liberal', 'progressive', 'broadminded', etc.

⑤ Lembede's views struck a chord in me. I, too, had been susceptible to paternalistic British colonialism and the appeal of being perceived by whites as 'cultured' and 'progressive' and 'civilized'. I was already on my way to being drawn into the black elite that Britain sought to create in Africa. That is what everyone from the regent to Mr Sidelsky had wanted for me. But it was an illusion. Like Lembede. I came to see the antidote as militant African nationalism.

[1] *ANC (abbr) = African National* Congress organization formed in 1912 to unite black South Africans against an oppressive white government
[10] *castigate sth.* strongly disapprove of sth.
[20] *Xhosas, Ndebeles, Tswanas* peoples in southern Africa
[28] *endeavour to do sth.* try hard to do sth.
[29] *eradicate sth.* get rid of sth.
[32] *dupe (infml)* sb. who is fooled into believing sth.
[36] *be susceptible to sth.* be vulnerable to sth.

2 Read paragraph ② again. Decide where Lembede ends each of the points he makes and mark this end with a vertical line. Read each separated point carefully, underlining any important words. Then tick the correct sentence ending:

Lembede's main idea is that Africans

☐ a) haven't been given opportunities.
☐ b) should change the way they think.
☐ c) have many heroes to lead them.

3 The topic of paragraph ② is Anton Lembede's views on Africanism. If you had to arrange the main points of his philosophy in a chart or table, which of the following formats – A or B – would you choose?

A

B

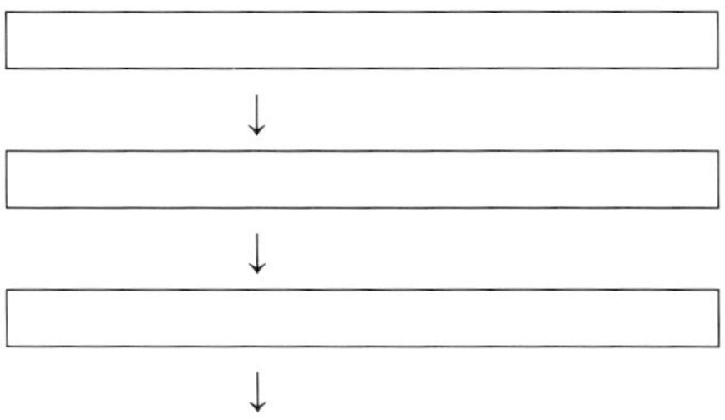

Discuss the reasons for your choice in class. Then, using the shape you have agreed on, write down Lembede's points in note form on a separate piece of paper or on the board.

Linking words and phrases
In order to follow the flow and meaning of a writer's argument, pay particular attention to the words or phrases used to connect individual thoughts and points. Linking words and phrases act as signals, telling the reader what is about to be expressed, for example:

However, …	→	contrast
Nonetheless, …	→	contrast
Nevertheless, …	→	contrast
Due to the fact that …	→	cause
Owing to the fact that …	→	cause
Consequently, …	→	result
That is to say, …	→	paraphrasing a previous point
Likewise, …	→	similarity
On the whole, …	→	conclusion
All things considered, …	→	conclusion

4 In paragraph ④, separate each point with a vertical line. Then look at the underlined linking phrases and decide which of the following simpler words could replace them without changing the meaning. (Several answers are possible.)

also • and • however • so • therefore

It is for that reason that ... – ______________________

for that purpose ... – ______________________

Read the paragraph again, using one of the simpler words you have chosen instead of the underlined phrases in order to follow the argument more easily. Then answer the following question:

According to Anton Lembede, why do imperialistic powers spend so much money on propaganda?

____

____

____

Which of the two tables in **3** roughly fits the shape of the argument in this paragraph?

5 For each paragraph of the text, find a suitable heading from the list below. There is one extra heading which you won't need to use.

a) Coming together as a nation

b) Getting ready for action

c) Avoiding a serious mistake

d) The peoples of Africa

e) An important meeting

f) Brainwashing the opposition

1 The following news reports are not as short as they could be. Underline the essential facts, then use them to write a new and shorter newsflash. Compare your answers in class.

a) A new number 12 bus, which was on its way to the centre of the city, crashed into a bus queue outside a big supermarket yesterday, seriously injuring three people including a baby boy.

____

____

____

b) In a protest against cuts in the education budget, 10,000 people including children, dressed in masks, shouting slogans and waving banners marched through the streets of New York to the Mayor's office yesterday.

____

____

____

Grasping the facts

A *news report* gives its readers the basic facts of a story very clearly, answering the '5 Ws': *who*, *what*, *when*, *where*, *why* and sometimes *how*. Descriptive details may be added.

Authors of *narrative texts* use more subtle techniques (and usually more words) to tell a story, develop their characters and describe events. The author may only infer or imply an important fact or feeling. In order to understand what is happening in a piece of narrative prose, you need to become efficient at separating fact from description and 'reading between the lines' to interpret what is being revealed.

2 Read the following descriptions and summarize what happens in your own words.

a) Maria sat in her bedroom on Sunday afternoon with her schoolbooks. She wrote an essay, worked out a maths problem and finished off her French translation.

Maria ______________________________

b) Tom's father stood up and threw the telephone bill on the floor, shouting and banging his fist on the table.

____

c) Jack waited, playing nervously with the diamond ring in his hand, as Ann gazed out across the lake. She slowly turned back to him, smiling, and kissed him softly. 'Yes, I will,' she whispered.

____

3 Coleman Silk, the main character of Philip Roth's novel *The Human Stain* (2000), has black parents but was born with very light coloured skin. He has been living his adult life as a "white" man in American society. He is married to Iris, whom he hasn't told about his true ancestry.

Read the first paragraph of the text and answer the questions.

And all the while he was driving home he was remembering the time he'd almost told Iris. It was after the twins were born. The family was now complete. They'd done it – he'd made it. With not a sign of his secret on any of his kids, it was as though he had been *delivered* from his secret. The exuberance that came of having pulled it off brought him to the very brink of giving the whole thing away. Yes, he would present his wife with the greatest gift he possessed: he would tell the mother of his four children who their father really was. He would tell Iris the truth. That was how excited and relieved he was, how solid the earth felt beneath his feet after she had their beautiful twins, and he took Jeff and Mikey to the hospital to see their new brother and sister, and the most frightening apprehension of them all had been eradicated from his life.

[3] *exuberance* great happiness
[8] *apprehension* fear
[9] *eradicate sth.* take sth. completely away, get rid of sth.

a) "With not a sign of his secret on any of his kids" (ll. 2–3) – explain what fact this tells the reader about Coleman Silk's children.

____

b) What had been Coleman's "most frightening apprehension" (l. 8)?

____

4 Now read the rest of the text.

But he never did give Iris that gift. He was saved from doing it – or damned to leave it undone – because of the cataclysm that befell a dear friend of hers, her closest associate on the art association board, a pretty, refined amateur watercolorist named Claudia McChesney, whose husband, owner of the county's biggest building firm, turned out to have quite a stunning secret of his own: a second family. For some eight years, Harvey McChesney had been keeping a woman years younger than Claudia, a bookkeeper at a chair factory over near the Taconic by whom he'd had two children, little kids aged four and six, living in a small town just across the Massachusetts line in New York State, whom he visited each week, whom he supported, whom he seemed to love, and whom nobody in the McChesneys' Athena household knew anything about until an anonymous phone call – probably from one of Harvey's building-trade rivals – revealed to Claudia and the three adolescent children just what McChesney was up to when he wasn't out on the job. Claudia collapsed that night, came completely apart and tried to slash her wrists, and it was Iris who, beginning at 3 a.m., with the help of a psychiatrist friend, organized the rescue operation that got Claudia installed before dawn in Austin Riggs, the Stockbridge psychiatric hospital. And it was Iris who, all the while she was nursing two newborns and mothering two preschool boys, visited the hospital every day, talking to Claudia, steadying her, reassuring her, bringing her potted plants to tend and art books to look at, even combing and braiding Claudia's hair, until, after five weeks – and as much a result of Iris's devotion as of the psychiatric program – Claudia returned home to begin to take the steps necessary to rid herself of the man who had caused all her misery.
In just days, Iris had got Claudia the name of a divorce lawyer up in Pittsfield and, with all the Silk kids, including the infants, strapped down in the back of the station wagon, she drove her friend to the lawyer's office to be absolutely certain that the separation arrangements were initiated and Claudia's deliverance from McChesney was under way. On the ride home that day, there'd been a lot of bucking up to do, but bucking people up was Iris's specialty, and she saw to it that Claudia's determination to right her life was not washed away by her residual fears.
'What a wretched thing to do to another person,' Iris said. 'Not the girlfriend. Bad enough, but that

happens. And not the little children, not even that – not even the other woman's little boy and girl, painful and brutal as that would be for any wife to discover. No, it's the secret – that's what did it, Coleman. That's why Claudia doesn't want to go on living. "Where's the intimacy?" That's what gets her crying every time. "Where is the intimacy," she says, "when there is such a secret?" That he could hide this from her, that he *would* have gone on hiding it from her – that's what Claudia's defenseless against, and that's why she still wants to do herself in.'

[24] *buck sb. up (infml)* encourage sb., cheer sb. up

Which of the following statements about the text is correct?

- [ ] a) Two men's secrets are discovered by their wives.
- [ ] b) Two men have been deceiving their wives.
- [ ] c) Two men tell their wives the truth.

Collecting information from a narrative text
When you are asked to extract information from a narrative text, first decide what range of information the task asks you to collect (e.g. actions, feelings – or both?). Use different colour pens to highlight different categories of relevant information.
Read direct speech carefully. You may need to describe it, or it may contain facts that need to be included in your answer.

5 Fill in the table according to the information given in the text.

Coleman Silk's secret:	**Harvey McChesney's secret:**
Claudia McChesney's reactions to discovering her husband's secret:	**Iris Silk's reactions to her friend's situation:**

6 Complete the following explanation:

Coleman Silk doesn't tell his wife about his secret because ______

1 a) 'How else might this be said?' Discuss the meaning of these adjectives and verbs in class:

inferior • adequate • essential • unusual
improve • protect • negotiate

b) 'What words might be used in a text about this topic?' Quickly list any words or phrases you can think of related to these nouns:

finance: money, ______________________

____

____

____

____

employment: ______________________

____

____

____

education: ______________________

____

____

____

> **Paraphrasing and wordfields**
> Reading tasks are often designed to test your ability to understand the topic idea so well that you can recognize related ideas in the text or recognize the original idea expressed in a different way.
> Therefore, read the question carefully, asking yourself how else something might be expressed (*paraphrases*, *synonyms*) and what words might be used on this topic in the text (*wordfields*).
> For instance, the fact that somebody has a *university degree* could mean that in the text in question you may come across the expressions *(university) graduate* or *(university) qualification*.
> If you are aware of and prepared for such related terms, you will be able to search the text for information more effectively.

2 Decide which of the alternatives corresponds best to the original statement. Explain your choice to the class.

a) 'Advertisements are designed to create a desire or need on the part of the consumer.'

Advertising makes people believe that products are necessary or wish-fulfilling. ☐

Adverts are created to attract people to things they want or consider necessary. ☐

> **Careful reading**
> Don't be tricked into choosing an area of text because it *seems* to contain what you are looking for. Use careful reading to check that it says *exactly* what you are looking for.

b) 'The reliability of statistics produced from street surveys depends on the honesty of the interviewees.'

If people interviewed in street surveys tell lies, the results will not be accurate. ☐

Street survey results cannot be relied on because people don't answer questions truthfully. ☐

3 Look at the statements in the left-hand column below. How else could they be phrased, and what different words and expressions might be used to do this?

Then read the text on the following page and decide whether Andrzej Klesyk or Tom Williams expresses them. In the table below, tick the right name and quote words from the text that confirm your choice.

A job applicant …	Klesyk	Williams	Evidence from the text
… should be truthful and courageous.			
… should have the outlook and positive energy to do well.			
… would not humiliate colleagues.			
… need not show proof of an in-depth study of their subject.			
… should be able to work easily with people of other races and religions.			
… should be able to work within planned costs.			

Flexibility and lateral thinking: What Europe's employers are looking for

What does Europe's elite want from a new generation of young workers? We asked [...] European industry leaders what they are looking for.

Andrzej Klesyk, president of PZU, one of the biggest insurance and financial institutions in Poland and central and eastern Europe

We are looking for those who think independently – those who keep their brains in their heads and not in their portable computers.

Today's secondary-school graduates can be sure of one thing: finishing university will not guarantee them work in their field of specialisation. They are practically guaranteed that before they retire they will have to change their work duties, specialisations and occupation several times.

So what kind of people are firms like PZU looking for? They are not looking for brilliant actuaries or brilliant marketers among students and freshly baked graduates, because they don't exist.

They are looking for people who in two-and-a-half or maybe even 10 years might become brilliant actuaries, managers and specialists of any kind. They are looking for potential which can be developed. They are looking for talent.

A truly talented candidate will be capable of holistic and original thinking, who can learn and select knowledge, can work in a team or network, and will know how to plan and execute his or her work to meet a schedule. They will be someone who has the ability to understand others and empathise with them, who is honest and brave, who can set ambitious targets and achieve them without stamping on the dignity of other people.

Tom Williams, executive vice-president, Programmes, at Airbus

We have a supply chain that stretches around the world, so we need people who are comfortable with multicultural environments. They have got to be able to mix, to work to deadlines on budget and technical performance. It is a combination of skills and not all of them are going to be able to have those skills.

The core of our hiring will be technical people, although we are not looking for them to have a specialist degree. We want them to have that basic skill but we don't want them to be like oven-cooked chickens when they come out of the education system. We want them to have an attitude and enthusiasm that will allow them to prosper. For me, that's almost as important as a qualification.

Gap-filling and matching tasks: using personal pronouns as clues
When you read short passages or sentences that have to be matched into a main text, look for pronouns and study them – the smallest words can help a lot. For example:
If a sentence says '*They* didn't know why *that* had caused the problem', you will want to know who 'they' are, as well as what the problem was and what caused it.
Looking in the text for the answers to your questions will help you match the sentence or passage with the right gap. In the example above, the text preceding the gap will probably mention people, the problem and the cause of the problem.

1 Skim the following text, ignoring the numbered gaps.

All together now? A portrait of race in Britain

Ade Akinbiyi, footballer

Ade Akinbiyi is a striker for Burnley Football Club. His parents are Nigerian.

After growing up in a mixed area like Hackney in London it was a shock to join Norwich football club. I was 16 at the time and moved into digs with an old lady in the middle of the countryside. I was probably the first black person she had ever looked after and I found it very difficult; she probably did, too. ① _____ My parents are Nigerian and I was used to eating jollof rice and chicken, but she cooked potatoes and roast dinners. I used to sneak home whenever I could.

Norwich was a very white place. To see another black person in those days was kind of a relief. I used to think about how other people might see me: what were they thinking? If I missed the bus to get to training I would walk instead of standing about waiting, because I was worried that people would question what a black guy was doing around the area. ② _____

When I started playing football my mum didn't like coming to watch me. She hated the abusive side of it, the swearing and shouting. Even today I am appalled by what people will shout in front of their children; of course the kids then grow up and carry on shouting it. The racism is still there.

③ _____

As a black man driving a nice car with tinted windows I get stopped by the police a lot. The famous phrase is, 'It fits your description, blah blah blah.' I'm never rude to them, because the ruder you are the longer it takes. ④ _____

Being a footballer, you move around a lot, and I've lived in all kinds of areas. I've always kept my principles about mixing with all people and all colours, but not everyone is like that. You get those people who talk to black people at work, but they don't want to socialise with them outside. ⑤ _____

Even within the black community there are differences. You get banter between Africans and West Indians. I had a team-mate at one of the clubs I played for who kept calling me 'African this' and 'African that'. I kept saying to the guy, 'You do know we're all from Africa?' That boy didn't know his roots. I don't think white people see any of that. ⑥ _____

I had a bunch of kids wanting to touch my hair at one club I played for. I didn't mind, I just let them do it because they had never felt hair like that before and they wanted to know what it was like.

⑦ _____ That's something that is very important to me. I love reading about history and other cultures and I've tried to pass that on to my son – we always watch the news together. He's mixed race and goes to school in a very white area, so when he was younger kids used to go up to him and say, 'How come you're dark skinned?' I had to sit him down and explain that a lot of parents don't teach their kids about these things.

[2] *digs (pl) (old-fashioned, infml)* rented room or rooms; lodgings
[4] *jollof rice* popular dish in parts of West Africa

2 Match the following sentences with the gaps in the text above. Work step by step (see the example given in a):

In each sentence, highlight or underline the personal pronoun(s). → Work together in class to identify what questions you need to find answers for in the text. → Decide which sentence fits each gap in the text. Add the appropriate letter in the text above. There is one extra sentence that you will not need to use.

a) "They might not have done, but I was young and insecure at the time."
→ They might not have done, but I was young and insecure at the time.
→ *Who* might not have done *what*? Who is 'I'? What time does the text refer to?
→ The sentence fits gap no. _____.

b) " It wasn't just race – there were cultural differences as well."

c) "It was the first step for them, finding out about someone else's culture."

d) "She wasn't racist but they didn't know that."

e) "Arguing with them is a waste of time."

f) "It happens in football, I'm not gonna lie."

g) "They just see black people as all the same, just like how people get Indians mixed up with Bengalis."

h) "It's quieter than it used to be and the police are trying to step up their work on it, but I don't think it will ever stop."

3 Work together in class to check your answers by re-asking and answering the questions you have identified.

Implication and inference: discovering meaning behind the words
Sometimes a writer means more than he or she explicitly says – they may even mean something else entirely. The additional or real meaning is hidden or *implied*. You, the reader, need to use your imagination and look at the meaning behind the words – you have to *infer* the meaning.
Writers of narrative texts may imply extra meaning in order to actively involve the reader in the story. In argumentative texts, implication is a powerful tool, used to lead the reader towards a conclusion that could be too controversial if expressly stated.
In everyday life, implication is often used when what we really want to say would seem rude or quarrelsome.

1 Discuss in class what is implied when ...

a) ... a friend is showing you a new dress and shoes she has just bought and you say, 'Oh, I love the shoes.'

b) ... a man shouts at the football referee: 'Have you ever read the rule book, mate?!'

c) ... two brothers are found beside a broken window by their mother and one brother says: 'I didn't do it.'

2 Read the following excerpt from Bill Bryson's humorous book *The Lost Continent – Travels in Small-Town America* (1989), then do the task below it.

I went straight out for dinner, but almost every place I approached was closed, and I ended up eating in a restaurant attached to a bowling alley – in clear violation of Bryson's third rule of dining in a strange town. Generally, I don't believe in doing things on principle – it's kind of a principle of mine – but I do have six rules of public dining to which I try to adhere. They are:

1. Never eat in a restaurant that displays photographs of the food it serves. (But if you do, never believe the photographs.)
2. Never eat in a restaurant with flock wallpaper.
3. Never eat in a restaurant attached to a bowling-alley.
4. Never eat in a restaurant where you can hear what they are saying in the kitchen.
5. Never eat in a restaurant that has live entertainers with any of the following words in their titles: Hank, Rhythm, Swinger, Trio, Combo, Hawaiian, Polka.
6. Never eat in a restaurant that has blood-stains on the walls.

In the event, the bowling-alley restaurant proved quite acceptable. Through the wall I could hear the muffled rumblings of falling bowling-pins and the sounds of Elmira's hairdressers and grease monkeys having a happy night out.

8 *flock wallpaper* textured wallpaper (Velourstapete)
16 *grease monkey (AE dated sl.)* car mechanic

What is the implied meaning behind each of Bryson's dining rules? Complete the table below. One implied meaning is not given – discuss in class what it may be and add it to the table.

Bill Bryson's rule number …	**Implied meaning**
	…, because it could be noisy and full of young people.
	…, because the staff or the type of customer it attracts could be dangerous.
	…, because the food might be old-fashioned and conventional.
	…, because the other diners will probably be 'cowboy' types with no taste.
	…, because the menu will probably not be very high-class or changed very often.
	______________________________ ______________________________

3 Read the following article about the BBC World Service, the world's largest international broadcaster. Then do the task below it.

My hero: the BBC World Service
By Jeremy Paxman

I don't suppose there are many heroes who wear a cardigan and cords. But that's how I imagine the BBC World Service, an ageing uncle who's seen it all. It has a style that makes understatement seem like flamboyance.

Yet I have never, ever, anywhere in the world, heard anyone say a bad word about the World Service. It is more trusted than its American equivalents, more lively than Deutsche Welle, more imitated (unsuccessfully) than any of them. It has a team of steady, dedicated and resourceful correspondents stationed around the world. Their probity is beyond doubt. Its television service puts its poverty on proud display every day.

How many people will be going to the barricades to save the Macedonian or Albanian services and the others now to be cut? Not many – most of us have no idea what they're saying. And as for the Caribbean, that's presumably a decision to leave the former colonies to the mercy of the American networks.

No journalistic service has a God-given right to exist for ever. But we are dealing here with something more. How many millions listen to the World Service in some form? A mere 241 million people, they say – the figures are so vast as not to mean very much. But it must be many more than will ever clap eyes on William Hague, listen to an ambassadorial speech or attend a Foreign Office leadership conference.

The World Service's misfortune was to be controlled by the Foreign Office. I can imagine the scene when the menacing note comes across from the Treasury. 'Good Heavens!' says the Permanent Secretary, 'they want us to save money. Anyone got any ideas?' No one suggests abandoning the pile on the Faubourg Saint-Honoré or recognising that perhaps the whole diplomatic service belongs to the days before email and the internet – the telephone even. Then a voice pipes up, 'I know, why don't we hand the BBC World Service over to the BBC and make it their problem?' 'Excellent,' says the PS. 'Shall we have a cup of tea?'

[1] *cardigan* knitted jacket
cords (pl) thick, ribbed, cotton trousers
[3] *flamboyance* quality of being unusually colourful
[7] *probity (fml)* honesty, integrity
[16] *William Hague* British politician, Foreign Secretary since 2010
[21] *Faubourg Saint-Honoré* street in Paris; (here) reference to the British embassy building in that street

In the writer's opinion, are the statements below true or false? In the right-hand column, quote or paraphrase words from the text that justify your answer.

Statement	**True**	**False**	**Evidence (1–10 words)**
The BBC World Service has years of experience and knowledge.	☐	☐	
The BBC World Service is a bright and vivid organization.	☐	☐	
US broadcasters in foreign countries do *not* provide an entertaining service.	☐	☐	
Part of the Foreign Office is *not* really useful anymore.	☐	☐	
The Foreign Office doesn't care about trying to save the BBC World Service.	☐	☐	

Dealing with unknown vocabulary

Don't panic if you come across an unknown word in a text. Use the context to help you work out its meaning:

- What kind of word is it – a verb, adverb, adjective, …?
- Identify the sense unit the word belongs to and study it.
- Are there any examples given in the surrounding text that could help you?
- Writers often use synonyms to emphasize a point. Could the word be a synonym for another word or idea that is before or after it in the text?
- Is there any further explanation of the word? Could the word be part of further explanation of something the writer has already said?
- Is the word compared to anything else in the sense unit?

Don't waste time trying to think of an equivalent word in German. Be satisfied with a general understanding of the word or idea.

1 Read the following passage from the book *Talk to the Hand* (2005) by Lynne Truss, a humorous book about rudeness in the modern world. The word in square brackets is a nonsense word. It represents a word you probably know.

> Surely one of the reasons that rudeness is such a huge issue for people today is that we worry about it more; it is a source of [*skisnal*]. We recount situations to each other, just to check our own reactions. 'Was that rude? I thought that was rude. Do you think that's rude? Oh thank goodness you agree with me, because I thought it was rude but then I thought maybe I was being over-sensitive.'

Work with a partner to find out what the real word is. Use the questions in the box to help you. Make notes explaining how you worked out your answer. You might start like this: 'The nonsense word seems to be a *verb/adverb/…*, because …'

Compare your answers and your notes in class.

2 Read the following short texts and decide what the highlighted words roughly mean. Tick the right box and be prepared to explain your answer in class.

> I have recently started playing badminton in the evenings, and last Thursday I managed to say, 'Sorry' nearly 500 times in a two-hour period, but here's the marvellous thing: I can still say it any time I want. Obviously, I wish I were as skilful at foot-work and bat-work as I am at apologising – but that's another story. What is so interesting, of course, is that we all apologise to each other; even the really good players. So quite a lot of energy that might be usefully diverted to running and hitting goes into consoling and exonerating, as well. 'No, not your fault! That shot was mine! I should have gone for that! You are completely in the clear! You really shouldn't apologise!' Every so often, we try to ban apology from the court, but we can't manage without it.

6 *console sb.* give comfort or sympathy to sb. who is unhappy

The word *exonerating* in line 6 is closest in meaning to

☐ a) ‘chatting in a friendly way’.

☐ b) ‘saying that somebody is not to blame’.

☐ c) ‘accusing others of making mistakes’.

> Why are people adhering less to the Ps and Qs? Where does that leave those of us who wince every day at the unspoken ‘thank you’ or the unthought-of ‘sorry’? Is there a strategy for cancelling the debt? Should we abandon our expectations of reciprocity? And isn’t it confusing that our biggest experience of formal politeness comes from the recorded voices on automated switchboards – who patently don’t mean it? ‘We are sorry we cannot connect you at this time,’ says the voice. But does it sound sorry? No, it doesn’t.

1 *adhere to the Ps and Qs* (here) watch one’s manners, be polite
wince (v) physically react as if in pain
3 *reciprocity* two-way exchange; action and reaction

The word *patently* in line 5 is closest in meaning here to

☐ a) ‘clearly’.

☐ b) ‘unhurriedly’.

☐ c) ‘rudely’.

KV 1 Skimming, scanning and careful reading

1 a), c), d): scanning; b), e), f): skimming
2 –
3

Subject	Book recommendation?	Why?
family watersports	A	300 swimming locations, a child wanting a paddle
global warming	G	current affairs, the environment
countryside animal farming	–	Cannot be C, which talks about an "urban garden".
fatherhood and divorce	D	advice for any father who finds himself going it alone
photo journalism	B	photographs, all the major events are captured
women's history	E	charts the progress of feminism
North Pole exploration	none	Cannot be F, which is about northern England.

KV 2 Skimming the text outline

1 Subject of the text: *India*
What does the reader learn about the subject? *India is a new global force.*
Text type: Could be a) expository, b) descriptive or c) argumentative.
Possible main focus of the text: a) economy, c) politics.
2 –
3 a) unbiased and factual
b) The text has aspects of both expository and argumentative texts.
c) First section: lines 0–27, second section: lines 26–52
d) First section: Old India / India before the change
Second section: New India / India after the change
e) India's old problematic bureaucracy: ll. 20–23
India's new problems: ll. 38–52
How India received outside help: ll. 24–27
The size of India's new economy: ll. 38–52
Nehru's politics: ll. 0–19
f) differences in living standards
4 1. d) – 2. a) – 3. e) –4. b) – 5. f) – 6. c)

KV 3 Scanning for information

1
a) –
b)

	Possible benefits of tourism	Possible disadvantages of tourism
Natural surroundings	• protects environment	• increases pollution
Employment	• creates jobs	• jobs only seasonal
Money	• brings in new money • minimal start-up costs	• local inflation • profits can 'leak' away to external suppliers and proprietors

Living conditions	• relatively clean • improves quality of life and well-being in local community • helps conserve national heritage	• strain on infrastructure and services • enhances social problems • overcrowding • traffic congestion

c) tourism's impacts
d) –

2
a) –
b) anxious, insecure, dissatisfied, inadequate. / With outdoor advertising, you cannot choose not to look at it.

KV 4 Topic, main idea and message

1 a) *He likes chocolate flavours.* No, because not all the food mentioned necessarily tastes of chocolate. *He doesn't like salty food.* No, because although the sentence says that Tom likes various sweet things, that does not automatically mean that he doesn't also like salty things.
b) Inferred message: He should stop eating sweet food / eat less sweet food because it is damaging his health.

2 a)

'Many big ideas have struggled over the centuries to dominate the planet,' begins the argument by Jonathon Porritt, government adviser and all-round environmental guru. 'Fascism. Communism. Democracy. Religion. But only one has achieved total supremacy. Its compulsive attractions rob its followers of reason and good sense. It has created unsustainable inequalities and threatened to tear apart the very fabric of our society. More powerful than any cause or even religion, it has reached into every corner of the globe. It is consumerism.'	topic
According to Porritt, the most senior adviser to the government on sustainability, we have become a generation of shopaholics. We are bombarded by advertising from every medium which persuades us that the more we consume, the better our lives will be. Shopping is equated with fun, fulfilment and self-identity. It is also, Porritt warns, *killing the planet*.	main idea
He argues, in an interview with the *Observer*, that merely switching to 'ethical' shopping is not enough. **We must shop less.**	message

b) Consumerism is killing the planet so we must shop less.

3 Lines 18–41: main idea
Lines 42–58: topic
Lines 59–77: message

4
- Learn to have more elegant, satisfying lives, consuming less
- Make sacrifices to reduce carbon emissions
- Use technology more intelligently and efficiently
- Enable people to see what the costs of living in a certain way really look like
- Get wiser to what happens when we enjoy the perks of this life

5 –

KV 5 The structure of argument

1

Before my mum got pregnant, we got on really well. She was always good company and helped me with lots of things.	background / setting the scene
But then the baby arrived about three months ago.	cause of problem
And mum doesn't seem to notice my existence any more!	problem
She is always busy and when the baby finally falls asleep, she disappears for a rest too.	details of problem
I can understand that she is tired. And I know the baby is helpless and relies on her for everything, so she doesn't really have a choice.	opposite viewpoint
But if things don't change soon, I think I'll be glad to get out! My home life just isn't the same anymore.	results, implications

2 a) The writer doesn't suggest a solution though he/she hints that things have to change (cf. l. 11).
b) He/She warns that if a solution isn't found, he/she might want to leave.

3 a) *Shakespeare in the Park* is a 50-year old tradition of performing Shakespeare's plays in New York. Its 'great ideal' is that entrance is free.
b) The words *erosion*, *stealth*, *risks*, *mere* hint at there being a problem.

4 Lines 1–10: background / setting the scene
Lines 11–20: problem, cause of the problem
Lines 21–33: details of the problem
Lines 34–41: opposite viewpoint
Lines 42–51: results/implications
Lines 52–66: background
Lines 67–83: results/implications

5 a) The problem is that the theatre is "moving away from the bedrock principle on which it was founded: that *all* tickets should be free" because it needs funds in order to operate and the organizers are giving free tickets to large corporations in return for their financial support – which, in effect, is selling these tickets.
b) The results/implications are that the entire institution is "cheapened", and what makes it uniquely valuable – its openness – is "eroded". Also, the corporate sponsors are "destroying the very egalitarianism they came to feed upon." A further implication is that, because of this, *Shakespeare in the Park* may "recede from our central stage to just a bunch of poor players signifying nothing" and may not be guaranteed another 50 years of existence.

KV 6 Isolating the argument

1 b) The warning is that British theatre is now in danger of praising anything from abroad while criticizing theatre made in Britain, i.e. creating a double standard in favour of foreign work.

2 a2, b1, c3

3 Descriptive examples in the text:
- Lines 7–15; writer's point: "Yet they do not rebel. They do not try to get out of the coop." (l. 15)
- Lines 17–27; writer's point: "Why? […] It's because 99.9 per cent of us are caught in the Rooster Coop just like those poor guys in the poultry market." (ll. 23–27)
- Lines 30–35; writer's point: "The trustworthiness of servants is the basis of the entire Indian economy." (l. 34–35)

4 c) – b) – a) – c)

KV 7 Breaking down paragraphs

1 –

2 Lembede said that Africa was a black man's continent, and it was up to Africans to reassert themselves and reclaim what was rightfully theirs. | He hated the idea of the black inferiority complex and castigated what he called the worship and idolization of the West and its ideas. The inferiority complex, he affirmed, was the greatest barrier to liberation. He noted that wherever the African had been given the opportunity, he was capable of developing to the same extent as the white man, citing such African heroes as Marcus Garvey, W.E.B. Du Bois and Haile Selassie. 'The colour of my skin is beautiful,' he said, 'like the black soil of Mother Africa.' | He believed blacks had to improve their own self-image before they could initiate successful mass action. | He preached self-reliance and self-determination, and called his philosophy Africanism. | We took it for granted that one day he would lead the ANC.

b)

3 Chart A works best, because the main points are contrasts (do's ↔ don't's, positives ↔ negatives).

In order to reclaim Africa, Africans should …	Africans shouldn't …
… reassert themselves. … reclaim what is rightfully theirs. … improve their own self image (to be ready to take action). … be self-reliant. … be self-determined.	… have an inferiority complex. … idolise the West and its ideas.

4 As Lembede later wrote in the newspaper Inkundla ya Bantu, an African newspaper in Natal:
The history of modern times is the history of nationalism. | Nationalism has been tested in the people's struggles and the fires of battle and found to be the only antidote against foreign rule and modern imperialism. | It is for that reason that the great imperialistic powers feverishly endeavour with all their might to discourage and eradicate all nationalistic tendencies among their alien subjects; | for that purpose huge and enormous sums of money are lavishly expended on propaganda against nationalism which is dismissed as 'narrow', 'barbarous', 'uncultured', 'devilish', etc. | Some alien subjects become dupes of this sinister propaganda and consequently become tools or instruments of imperialism, for which great service they are highly praised by the imperialistic power and showered with such epithets as 'culture', 'liberal', 'progressive', 'broadminded', etc.
Both underlined phrases can be replaced by the words *so* or *therefore*.
Imperialistic powers spend much money on propaganda in order to eradicate nationalistic tendencies in their subjects, because nationalism threatens foreign rule.
Chart B best fits the shape of the argument in this paragraph because the arrows roughly represent the way the points in the argument are linked (cause → effect).

5 3a – 2b – 5c – (d is not used) – 1e – 4f

KV 8 Identifying fact in fiction

1 a) A bus crashed into a bus queue yesterday, seriously injuring three people including a baby.
b) 10,000 people, including children, marched through New York yesterday to protest against cuts in the education budget.

2 a) Maria was doing her homework on Sunday afternoon.
b) Tom's father was angry about the telephone bill.
c) Ann agreed to marry Jack.

3 a) His children were born white.
b) He had been afraid that his children would be born with black features, thereby betraying his secret.

4 b)

5 Coleman Silk's secret:
He is pretending to be white, although his parents are black. He hasn't told his wife or children.
Harvey McChesney's secret:
For eight years he has had a second family who he has been visiting every week.
Claudia McChesney's reactions to discovering her husband's secret:

She has a nervous breakdown and tries to kill herself. Later, she wants to get a divorce. She cries frequently.
Iris Silk's reactions to her friend's situation:
She organizes psychiatric treatment for her and regularly visits her when she is in hospital. She encourages her to get a divorce.

6 Coleman Silk doesn't tell his wife about his secret because he realizes how hurt/upset she would be about him keeping a secret from her and that she might divorce him.

KV 9 Paraphrasing and wordfields

1 a) Individual responses
b) Individual entries

2 a) First alternative ("Advertising makes people believe that products are ncessary or wish-fulfilling.")
b) First alternative ("If people interviewed in street surveys tell lies, the results will not be accurate.")

3 Who says that the right kind of job applicant:

A job applicant ...	Klesyk	Williams	Evidence from the text
... should be truthful and courageous.	✓		"honest and brave" (l. 19)
... should have the outlook and positive energy to do well.		✓	"attitude and enthusiasm that will allow them to prosper" (ll. 28–29)
... would not humiliate colleagues.	✓		"without stamping on the dignity of other people" (ll. 19–20)
... need not show proof of an in-depth study of their subject.		✓	"we are not looking for them to have a specialist degree" (ll. 26–27)
... should be able to work easily with people of other races and religions.		✓	"comfortable with multicultural environments" (ll. 22–23)
... should be able to work within planned costs.		✓	"on budget" (l. 23)

KV 10 Pronouns as clues

1 –

2

a) "They might not have done, but I was young and insecure at the time."
→ *Who* might not have done *what*? (Answer: People might not have questioned what a black guy was doing around the area.) Who is 'I'? (Answer: The writer, Ade Akinbiyi.) What time does the text refer to? (Answer: The time when Akinbiyi was living in Norwich.) → 2

b) "It wasn't just race – there were cultural differences as well." → *What* wasn't just race? (Answer: The difficulties between the writer and the old lady in his digs.) → 1

c) "It was the first step for them, finding out about someone else's culture." → *What* was the first step? (Answer: Touching the writer's hair.) *For whom?* (Answer: For the children.) → 7

d) "She wasn't racist but they didn't know that." → *Who* wasn't racist? Who are 'they'? → There is no context that answers both these questions; the sentence fits into none of the gaps.

e) "Arguing with them is a waste of time." → Arguing with *whom* is a waste of time? (Answer: The police.) → 4

f) "It happens in football, I'm not gonna lie." → *What* happens in football? (Answer: People talking to black people at work but not socialising with them outside.) → 5

g) "They just see black people as all the same, just like how people get Indians mixed up with Bengalis." → *Who* just sees black people as all the same? (Answer: White people.) → 6

h) "It's quieter than it used to be and the police are trying to step up their work on it, but I don't think it will ever stop." → *What* is quieter than it used to be? (Answer: The situation at football matches.) *What* are the police trying to step up their work on? *What* will never stop? (Answer: Racism.) → 3

3 –

KV 11 Reading behind the words

1 a) You don't like the dress.
b) The man thinks that the referee doesn't know what she/he is doing, that she/he isn't doing her/his job properly.
c) The other brother did it.

2 3 – 6 – 2 – 5 – 1 – …
Suggested reason for remaining rule 4: … because realizing how the food is prepared may put you off eating it.

3

Statement	True	False	Evidence (1–10 words)
The BBC World Service has years of experience and knowledge.	✓		"an ageing uncle who's seen it all." (l. 2)
The BBC World service is a bright and vivid organisation.		✓	"has a style that makes understatement seem like flamboyance." (ll. 2–3)
US networks in foreign countries do *not* provide an entertaining service.	✓		… leave the former colonies "to the mercy of the American networks." (ll. 11–12)
Part of the Foreign office is *not* really useful anymore.	✓		… the whole diplomatic service belongs to the days before email and the internet – the telephone even." (ll. 20–21)
The Foreign Office doesn't care about trying to save the BBC World Service.	✓		Hand it to the BBC "and make it their problem" (l. 22)

KV 12 Unknown vocabulary

1 *skisnal* = anxiety
Kind of word: noun.
Further explanation: The nonsense word seems to be a further explanation of worrying about rudeness – rudeness is a source of *skisnal*/worrying.
Examples given: The person speaking is 'worrying'.
Synonym: A noun that has the meaning of worrying could be 'worry' but the writer would probably not repeat him or herself in that way. Another noun for worrying is *anxiety*.

2 First text: b). The answer is found in the examples. The speaker says 'not your fault' and 'you are completely in the clear', both of which show that the other person is not to blame.
Second text: a). Answer b) is not logical in the context and could reflect confusion with the word 'patiently'. Answer c) does not fit either, since the recorded voice speaks politely.

KV1: The Guardian Newspaper books © Guardian News & Media Ltd 2012
KV2: Aditya Chakrabortty: "How did India do it? The rise of a new global force", *The Guardian*, 14.8.07 © Guardian News & Media Ltd 2007
KV 3: Kerry Godfrey / Jackie Clarke, *The Tourism Development Handbook*, Thomson 2000 (reprinted 2003), with permission from Cengage Learning Rights and Content Reuse; Neal Lawson: "Assaulted in broad daylight", *The Guardian Weekly*, 27.4.12 © Guardian News & Media Ltd 2012
KV 4: David Smith: "Stop shopping … or the planet will go pop", *The Observer*, 8.4.07 © Guardian News & Media Ltd 2007
KV 5: Jason Farago: "The erosion by stealth and wealth of Shakespeare in the Park's great ideal", *The Guardian*, 7.6.12 © Guardian News & Media Ltd 2012
KV 6: Michael Billington: "X Is for Xenophobia", *The Guardian*, 22.5.12 © Guardian News & Media Ltd 2012; Aravind Adiga, *The White Tiger* © Caitlin Ingham / Literary Agency David Godwin
KV 7: From *Long Walk to Freedom* by Nelson Mandela. © 1994 by Nelson Rolihlahla Mandela. By permission of Little, Brown and Company. All rights reserved.
KV 8: Extract from *The Human Stain* by Philip Roth. Copyright © Philip Roth, 2000, used by permission of the Whylie Agency (UK) Limited
KV 9: "Flexibility and lateral thinking: What Europe's employers are looking for", *The Guardian*, 31.5.12 © Guardian News & Media Ltd 2012
KV 10: "All together now? A portrait of race in Britain" (Ade Akinbiyi, interviewed by Anna Kessell), *The Observer*, 18.1.2009 © Guardian News & Media Ltd 2009
KV 11: Bill Bryson, *The Lost Continent* © Bill Bryson, reprinted by permission of the author; Jeremy Paxman: "My Hero: the BBC World Service", *The Guardian*, 29.01.2011 © Guardian News & Media Ltd 2011
KV 12: © Lynne Truss, *Talk to the Hand. The Utter Bloody Rudeness of Everyday Life*, Fourth Estate Ltd. (2010)

Verfasserinnen: Sabine Brumby-Hartogh, Göttingen, Heidrun Krause, Braunschweig, und Ulrike Schuh-Fricke, Braunschweig (Einleitung und beratende Mitwirkung); Liz Stolls, Petra, Lesvos, Griechenland (Kopiervorlagen)

Verlagsredaktion: Martina Krause, Dr. Christian v. Raumer

Design und technische Umsetzung: MatMil Translations & Desktop Publishing, Berlin

Umschlaggestaltung: sans serif, Berlin

Reading

Teaching SKILLS

www.cornelsen.de

1. Auflage, 1. Druck 2013

Druck: H. Heenemann, Berlin

ISBN 978-3-06-033241-0

Inhalt gedruckt auf säurefreiem Papier aus nachhaltiger Forstwirtschaft.